BEAVERS

by Matt Lilley

Cody Koala
An Imprint of Pop!
popbooksonline.com

abdobooks.com
Published by Pop!, a division of ABDO, PO Box 398166, Minneapolis,
Minnesota 55439. Copyright © 2019 by POP, LLC. International copyrights
reserved in all countries. No part of this book may be reproduced in any
form without written permission from the publisher. Pop!™ is a trademark
and logo of POP, LLC.

Printed in the United States of America, North Mankato, Minnesota.

092018
012019
THIS BOOK CONTAINS
RECYCLED MATERIALS

Cover Photo: iStockphoto
Interior Photos: iStockphoto, 9, 19 (top), 19 (bottom right); Shutterstock
Images, 5, 6, 7, 11, 12, 15, 16, 19 (bottom left), 20

Editor: Charly Haley
Series Designer: Laura Mitchell

Library of Congress Control Number: 2018949241

Publisher's Cataloging-in-Publication Data

Names: Lilley, Matt, author.
Title: Beavers / by Matt Lilley.
Description: Minneapolis, Minnesota: Pop!, 2019 | Series: Pond animals |
    Includes online resources and index.
Identifiers: ISBN 9781532162046 (lib. bdg.) | ISBN 9781641855754 (pbk) |
    ISBN 9781532163104 (ebook)
Subjects: LCSH: Beavers--Juvenile literature. | Mammals--Behavior--
    Juvenile literature. | Pond animals--Juvenile literature.
Classification: DDC 599.37--dc23

Hello! My name is

Cody Koala

Pop open this book and you'll find QR codes like this one, loaded with information, so you can learn even more!

Scan this code* and others like it while you read, or visit the website below to make this book pop.

popbooksonline.com/beavers

*Scanning QR codes requires a web-enabled smart device with a QR code reader app and a camera.

Table of Contents

Chapter 1

Land and Water

Beavers are large **rodents**.

They spend time on land

and in water.

Watch a video here!

Beavers go on land to
get food. They eat bark,
small branches, and plants.

Beavers have strong,

sharp teeth.

Beaver teeth are always growing. Chewing on trees keeps their teeth from getting too long.

Beavers love water! Their back feet are webbed like ducks' feet. This helps them swim. Their thick fur keeps them dry.

Chapter 2

Predators

When beavers are on the land, other animals might try to eat them. These other animals are called **predators**. Wolves and bears can eat beavers.

Learn more here!

Beavers are safe in the water. When a beaver sees a predator, it slaps its tail on the water. This warns other beavers of danger. Then the beaver swims to safety.

Chapter 3

Beaver Families

A beaver house is called a lodge. Beavers make lodges out of logs, sticks, and mud. Most beavers live in a family.

Learn more here!

A beaver family can have a mom, dad, brothers, and sisters. Young beavers are called **kits**. Older kits help take care of the younger kits.

Baby beavers stay inside the lodge until they are about a month old.

Builders

Beavers are really busy. They cut down trees. They build lodges and **dams**.

Beavers keep branches underwater to eat during the winter.

Complete an activity here!

When a beaver makes a dam on a stream, the dam blocks the water. This turns the stream into a beaver pond. A beaver pond is a **habitat** for other plants and animals.

Making Connections

Text-to-Self

Have you ever seen a beaver? If not, have you seen another animal in the wild?

Text-to-Text

Have you read another book about a different animal? How is that animal similar to a beaver? How is it different?

Text-to-World

Beavers live near trees and water. Are there many trees near where you live? Are there any lakes or rivers?

Glossary

dam – something that holds back water.

habitat – a place for a plant or animal to live.

kit – a young beaver.

predator – an animal that hunts and eats other animals.

rodent – a type of animal that has a single pair of strong teeth.

Index

Online Resources

popbooksonline.com

Thanks for reading this Cody Koala book!

Scan this code* and others like it in this book, or visit the website below to make this book pop!

popbooksonline.com/beavers

*Scanning QR codes requires a web-enabled smart device with a QR code reader app and a camera.